POLICE

lpin

EDGE
W
FRANKLIN
WATTS

LONDON·SYDNEY

First published in 2010 by
Franklin Watts
338 Euston Road
London NW1 3BH

Franklin Watts Australia
Level 17/207 Kent Street
Sydney NSW 2000

Series editor: Adrian Cole
Art director: Jonathan Hair
Design: Simon Borrough
Picture research: Luped

Acknowledgements:
67photo / Alamy: 11b; Alisdair Macdonald / Rex Features: 29t; Andrew Brookes / Corbis: 31; Anlogin / Shutterstock: Front Cover; Baxternator / iStockphoto: 14, 45; Chris Howes / Wild Places Photography / Alamy: 12; Cole Thornton / fotolia: 24, 44c; CPS / PA Archive: 37; cynoclub / fotolia: 18; David Keith Jones / Alamy: 13b; David Lentz / iStockphoto: 7t; Eric Hood / iStockphoto: 9tr; Fedor Kondratenko / iStockphoto: 36b; Flame / Alamy: 39r; George Cairns / iStockphoto: 7b; George Cairns / iStockphoto: Endpapers; Bill Greenblatt / Corbis: 32; HotNYCNews / Alamy: 23t; imagebroker / Alamy: 17t; Ivan Gusev / fotolia: 9c; Janine Wiedel Photolibrary / Alamy: 16; Jason Bye / Rex Features: 29b; Jochen Tack / Alamy: 3, 10, 21t, 25t, 38; John McCombe / Getty Images: 28; Jose Miguel Gomez / Reuters / Corbis: 36c; KPA / Zuma / Rex Features: 27b; Leeuwtje / iStockphoto: 27t, 44t; Luo Li / Redlink / Corbis: 19t; Michael Matthews / Alamy: 34, 35t, 35b; Mike Meadows / AP Photo: 40b; 40c, 41; Misha Gordon / Alamy: 15b; moodboard / fotolia: 19b; Natsukashi / Alamy: 9tl; NDP / Alamy: 11t; Nick Scott / Alamy: 20; NY Daily News Archive / Getty Images: 33b; Peter Kim / dreamstime.com: 39l; Rex Features: 30; Romeo Gacad / AFP / Getty Images: 33c; Scott Stuart / iStockphoto: 17b; Sean Boggs / iStockphoto: 9b; Seth Wenig / AP Photo: 22; Shaun Cunningham / Alamy: 26; Shout / Alamy: 15t, 21b; Shout / Rex Features: 25c; Stephen Fore / fotolia: 9tc; Sunpix People / Alamy: 13t; Tillsonburg / iStockphoto: 6b; Tony Savino / Corbis: 23c; Uden Graham / Redlink / Corbis: 8b.

A CIP catalogue record for this book is available from the British Library.

Dewey number: 363.2

ISBN: 978 0 7496 9349 7

Printed in China

Franklin Watts is a division of Hachette Children's Books,
an Hachette UK company.
www.hachette.co.uk

Contents

Words highlighted in the text can be found in the glossary.

Meet the police

The police play an important role in tackling crime and keeping us safe. Within the police force there are many different jobs that use a wide range of skills.

"It's almost like a calling. If I'm in uniform, I'm excited. I love what I do."

Rob Williams, Chief of Springfield Police Department, Illinois, USA

AF FACTS

The world's first true police force was formed in 1829 in London. It was created by Robert Peel. The members of this new police force were called 'Peelers' or 'Bobbies' after their founder.

Police tape is used to keep people away from a crime scene.

POLICE LINE DO NOT CROSS   POLICE LINE

CROSS

POLICE

This police officer has stopped a suspect car.

Most police officers wear uniforms and patrol on foot or in cars. They are based at local police stations, where an inspector or sheriff is in command.

Police forces have different departments. Some officers become dog handlers. Others join the traffic police and become highly skilled pursuit drivers.

Police forces also have detectives who work hard to solve crimes. They have often served as uniformed officers and know the local area well.

This police officer on foot patrol is talking to an officer on patrol in a car.

Personal gear

All police officers carry special equipment to help them with their jobs. Most also wear uniforms. These make them easy to identify.

Police equipment varies depending on the police officer's role, but most carry a baton and handcuffs. These are carried on a duty belt or outer vest. Most police officers also carry a communications radio. This is used to keep in contact with the police station and other police officers. In some countries, officers also carry a torch and disposable gloves.

"I'd like to see all [UK] officers armed. The threat faced by police officers today is very real and it is getting worse."
John O'Connor, former commander of Scotland Yard's flying squad

These police officers are on patrol in Hong Kong International airport.

These police officers are wearing high visibility jackets.

Communications radio

Handcuffs

Police baton

The police in many countries carry handguns. They are held in a holster on the duty belt. In some places, police officers carry submachine-guns. 'Non-lethal' weapons, such as CS spray and tasers, are also used by police forces in countries such as Canada, France, the UK and the USA.

AF FACTS

Tasers are hand-held weapons designed to stop dangerous suspects. The taser is held like a handgun, but it doesn't fire bullets. Instead, it passes an electric current that stops a person's muscles working and causes extreme pain.

Taser

Highway patrols

The main job of highway patrols and other traffic police is to make sure car users drive safely. They also check drivers have the correct documents, such as a driving licence.

AF FACTS

More than one car is often needed to stop suspect cars. Police box in drivers by using two or more cars. They force them to slow down and stop. Special spiked 'stop sticks' or 'stingers' can also be laid down to puncture a suspect's car tyres.

Police traffic units put up signs that warn other road users that there has been an accident.

ACTION STATS

Every year, more than 1 million people in the USA are stopped and arrested for drink driving, or driving under the influence of drugs.

"The reality is alcohol affects everybody differently. There is no safe limit and the message is to not do it at all."
Mick Giannasi, Chief Constable of Gwent Police, Wales, talks about drink driving

Traffic patrol cars are designed to be easy to see and hear, with a light bar on the roof and a noisy siren. Traffic police are often the first to arrive at a road traffic accident (RTA). Officers help to direct other road users around the RTA. Traffic police also pursue suspects at high speed. They have advanced driver training and specially modified cars. They can arrest drivers suspected of driving under the influence of drugs or alcohol, and take their vehicle.

Police officers use a breathalyser to test for alcohol levels.

Bike patrols

Police motorbikes like these ones have powerful engines. These are Honda ST1300s in use by Gwent Police in Wales.

Officers in some police traffic units use motorbikes. They are particularly useful in built-up areas and other places where cars may find it hard to get through. Police bicycles are also used to patrol smaller areas.

AF FACTS

Different police forces use different motorbikes. In the UK, many forces use BMW RT Series bikes or Honda ST1300s. Harley-Davidson bikes are used in the USA and Canada, alongside other makes. They are also used by some branches of the German police.

Police motorbikes are used a lot by city police forces. Police officers can reach crime scenes quickly, even during rush hour when there are lots of cars on the roads. Other police forces use off-road motorbikes or all-terrain vehicles (ATVs, see page 17) to patrol areas of tough **terrain**.

This police officer is riding a Harley-Davidson police motorbike in Utah, USA.

Police bicycles are fitted with lights and a siren – just like other police vehicles. They can move quickly over short distances, either through busy traffic or where vehicles cannot go. The bicycles are usually specially modified mountain bikes made by Trek, Specialized or Cannondale.

These French police officers are on patrol in Amiens.

Police vehicles

Police forces around the world use different vehicles. Police cars are the most important of these, but they are not all the same.

Most police cars have police markings, such as high-visibility strips, flashing lights and a loud siren. Underneath the bonnet, some cars also have special engines that generate lots of power.

 This police 4x4 has pulled over a car driving dangerously on an icy road.

Police officers use cars when on patrol. They can be used to transport one or two suspects back to the police station. Four-wheel-drive (4x4) vehicles, such as the Chevrolet Tahoe or Ford Explorer, are often used in **rural** areas. They can travel easily across rough ground on farms and dirt tracks.

"It's not just a police car, it's an office-on-wheels for police officers."
Nick Mohamed, police officer, Ontario, Canada

Some police cars are unmarked. They are used for undercover operations. But even these cars have sirens and lights (usually hidden behind the radiator grille).

Unmarked cars look like normal cars.

AF FACTS

The Lamborghini Gallardo is the world's fastest police car. It is used by the Italian police in Rome. Rome's police force has two of these cars, worth £140,000 each. The Lamborghini Gallardo can go from 0-60mph in 4.1 seconds and has a top speed of 197mph.

The Lamborghini Gallardo is used by the Italian traffic police (Polizia Stradale) for motorway patrols.

Police units across the world also use vans, boats and other specialised vehicles to help them keep law and order.

When large numbers of police need to be moved, for example to control **demonstrations**, they are carried in vans. Other police vans are used to detain suspects and transport them to the police station. Specialised police vans also transport police dogs and **surveillance** equipment.

A man is handcuffed and led to a waiting police van. Police vans often have holding cages in the back.

AF FACTS

In Britain, where few police officers carry guns, some police forces have Armed Response Vehicles, or ARVs. They are used by Tactical Firearms Units to reach emergency situations quickly.

ATVs, or all-terrain vehicles, are fast, four-wheel-drive vehicles. Police units in Australia use ATVs to patrol many different areas, including sandy beaches and rocky Outback areas.

Police boats patrol waterways, including rivers and coastal areas. They are used to board and investigate suspicious vessels and combat **smuggling**. They may also be used to chase fleeing suspects or to help rescue people who have fallen in the water.

This police ATV patrols a sandy beach in Lanzarote, the Canary Islands.

Police boats are fast which helps them to pursue suspects on the river.

"You come up in a strange or unknown boat and you're very likely to be boarded and checked."
Steve Trusler, police boat driver, UK Metropolitan Police Marine Support Unit

Dog Squad

Dogs are an important tool in modern policing. They are fast and have a powerful sense of smell. Police dogs can be trained to do many different jobs.

During the dog training process, police officers wear protective gear and pretend to be suspects.

"To them, it's a game. They know at the end of it they're going to get a reward."
Brian Ziolkovski, dog handler,
Old Saybrook Police,
Connecticut, USA

AF FACTS

Police dog handlers are specially trained. Most police dogs live at home with their handlers. A police dog's working life is around eight years. Once retired, dogs normally live as their handler's pet.

18

Some police dogs are trained to chase suspects on the run and bring them to the ground. Dogs are faster than even the quickest person. Police dogs are trained to chase and attack on command.

These German Shepherd dogs are being trained to chase suspects by Chengdu Police in China.

Most police dogs are German Shepherds. However, other breeds, such as Labradors and spaniels are also used as sniffer dogs. They are trained to sniff out substances. Some are taught to search for drugs, and others for explosives. There are even dogs that sniff out banknotes.

This sniffer dog has found drugs in a bag dumped by a suspect.

Search and rescue

Search and rescue is a very specialised job. Officers help to find missing people, often in dangerous places.

Search and rescue officers may need to look for missing hikers in hilly areas during a storm. They also **abseil** down cliffs to help rescue injured climbers. They may even dive into freezing cold lakes to look for murder weapons, such as knives. They use 4x4 vehicles and can call rescue helicopters.

A Land Rover 4x4 rescue unit.

"It's not all about recovering bodies, but it is something you have to do – often in tough diving conditions."

Andy Clark, police diver, UK

*This police diver from Germany is wearing **scuba** gear during a lake search.*

Not everyone can be a search and rescue officer. They need special skills above and beyond everyday policing. Officers can be trained to use police sniffer dogs and diving equipment. Once they have shown their fitness and abilities they may join a search and rescue unit. They then need to be 'on call' and ready to respond 24 hours a day.

Police sniffer dogs, such as this bloodhound, are mainly used to find missing people.

Mission: Haiti 2010

On 12 January, 2010, the Caribbean country of Haiti was struck by a massive earthquake. The epicentre of the earthquake was just outside the capital city, Port-au-Prince.

A police officer prepares to travel to Haiti.

The first search and rescue teams arrived within hours. Much of the city was devastated, with many thousands of people trapped under collapsed buildings. Police search and rescue officers from New York, USA, and Spain joined forces with firefighters and other experts.

ACTION-STATS

Within five days of the earthquake, 43 different search and rescue teams arrived in Haiti. Between them, they had 1,739 search and rescue experts and 161 sniffer dogs.

These Chinese police officers are part of a United Nations (UN) operation in Haiti in 2010.

They used search and rescue dogs to look for survivors (right). In the days that followed, more than 100 people were discovered still alive, and they were rescued from the rubble. Sadly, thousands of bodies were also recovered. People were killed instantly by falling buildings when the earthquake struck, or died later before rescuers could reach them.

"No matter the cause, our training kicks in. It doesn't matter if [the disaster] is man made or natural. That's not what it's about for us."
James Cole, New York City police detective and search and rescue officer

Air wing

The air wing is made up of special police aircraft, police officers and pilots. They play an important part in crime control.

"Criminals can now be caught on land and from the sky. [The Air Wing] has assisted us in providing a safer Victoria."
Inspector Bruce Thomas, Victoria Police Air Wing, Australia

Police helicopters assist officers on the ground and can see whole areas where incidents and crimes are in progress.

This police helicopter uses its cameras to record events on the ground.

AF FACTS

Australia's New South Wales Police Air Wing is one of the oldest air wing units in the world. It was set up in 1946 to transport detectives and investigators to crime scenes in the Outback and other remote places.

Air wing officers watching from the air use their radios to send information. They can tell police on the ground which way a suspect is driving or running, to make sure that he or she is caught. Most police air wing units use helicopters, although a few use aeroplanes too.

Inside the helicopter, the pilot uses night-vision goggles to help him fly in the dark.

"As part of law enforcement, as part of emergency response, the value [of police helicopters] cannot be overestimated."

Michael D. Bissonnette, mayor of Chicopee, Massachusetts, USA

AF FACTS

Most police helicopters are fitted with both video and thermal imaging cameras. Video cameras are used to film by day, while thermal imaging cameras film at night (left). Thermal imaging cameras work by picking up sources of heat, such as human bodies. They can be used to track fleeing suspects in total darkness.

Mounted police

Now that police forces have cars and other vehicles, it might seem strange that they still use horses. But in fact, mounted police are very important. They do jobs officers on foot or in cars cannot do so well.

AF FACTS

The world's most famous mounted police are the Canadian Mounties (right). When the force began in the late 1800s nearly all of its officers rode on horseback. Today, only a small number actually ride horses, but the name Mounties has stuck and is used for all Canadian police.

Police horses are especially useful in rural and wilderness areas (right). In the USA, they are used to patrol many National Parks. They are also used along the USA-Mexico border in areas where motor vehicles cannot go. Police horses are commonly used in countries where there are few roads.

The second major job mounted police units carry out is keeping public order. They are used at demonstrations, football matches and other places where large crowds gather. Officers on horseback are better able than those on foot to see what is going on in crowds. They can quickly spot problems, such as crushes or violent behaviour.

"You have a real presence when you're nine feet tall. Nobody wants to go up against a 635-kilogramme animal."
Inspector Luis Del Rio, director of the mounted unit in Providence, Rhode Island, USA

These police horses are being used to break up a riot.

Homicide squad

The job of the homicide squad is to investigate suspicious deaths. Most of the people who work in homicide squads are detectives. They gather evidence to try to work out how and why people were killed.

"Murder is a brutal, ugly thing: 80% or 90% of the time it involves narcotics [drugs] or alcohol in one way or another."

A Chicago homicide detective

Most people know about detectives and homicide squads from TV programmes. Being a real police detective isn't very showbiz – it's hard work, with long hours and night shifts. Whenever a person is killed or found dead in suspicious circumstances, the homicide squad is brought in.

Detectives and other officers collect physical evidence at a murder scene.

Detectives spend time at the police station recording evidence.

Detectives also interview anyone who may have seen or heard anything – called witnesses. This often means talking to hundreds of people. Detectives then use the physical clues and witness accounts to try to solve the crime.

ACTION STATS

In London there are three or four homicides every week. Although this sounds like a lot, there are eight times as many homicides per 100,000 people in New York. The world's worst city for homicides is Washington DC, which has 33 times as many homicides per 100,000 people than London does.

Detectives brief uniformed officers before raiding a suspect's home.

Crime scene investigators

Crime scene investigators are called to places where crimes have taken place. They are forensic experts who collect evidence and make sure that the crime scene is not disturbed by other people.

The job of a crime scene investigator is very important in helping to solve crimes. He or she collects evidence from where the crime happened. This evidence may be used to build a case against a suspect in **court**. Crime scene investigators look for physical evidence, such as hairs, blood, footprints,

AF FACTS

In some countries, such as Britain, crime scene investigators are known as scene of crime officers (SOCOs). In 2009 they were called to 1,500 crime scenes and processed around 500,000 DNA samples.

fingerprints or fibres of clothing. They also take photographs of the scene. Later, they may take saliva samples from suspects to test their **DNA** (see right) and compare it against DNA found at the crime scene.

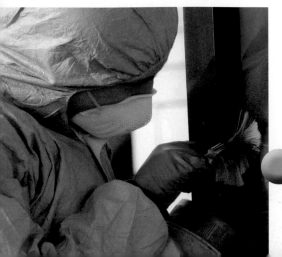

A SOCO dusts for fingerprints that may have been left after a violent attack.

"It can take hours to get evidence. You may be away from your family. You may have to go through uncomfortable situations."
Leona Williams, forensic technician, Broward County, South Florida, USA

This crime scene investigator is checking a knife for blood.

AF FACTS

DNA is the blueprint needed for living things, such as human beings. DNA is unique to an individual and can be used to trace people – like a fingerprint.

Drug task force

Illegal drugs are a major cause of crime in the world today. The job of a police drug task force is to investigate the supply and trafficking (movement) of illegal drugs.

A DEA agent checks a chemical used to make drugs found at a house.

A police drug task force deals with a particular type of crime: the trade in illegal drugs, such as heroin and cocaine. Most police forces have some detectives who work in their drug task force full time. Other detectives and uniformed officers are drafted in from other police departments to help with large cases.

AF FACTS

Drug task force detectives often work undercover, posing as buyers to gather the information needed to make arrests. These undercover officers are sometimes armed for self-protection. They may also wear a hidden microphone and radio transmitter.

Although they all do the same job, drug task forces differ around the world. In some countries, such as the UK and Australia, they work as units within county or state police forces. In other countries, they work as part of a larger organisation. Scotland has the Scottish Drug Enforcement Agency, while the USA has its own Drug Enforcement Administration (DEA).

Officers of the Philippine Drug Enforcement Agency (PDEA) remove equipment used to make drugs from a house in San Rafael.

"It can be a really complicated job. It requires a person with integrity and a lot of common sense."
Sheriff Donnie Tinnell, Bullitt County, Kentucky, USA

These 'build-a-bear' kits were used by drug traffickers to smuggle heroin.

Organised crime unit

Crime carried out on a large scale, where criminals work together, is called organised crime. The police create organised crime units to gather information and identify and arrest the people involved.

"Twenty-first century crime is a global business that doesn't respect borders. SOCA's links with international partners mean criminals who try to cause harm to the UK have nowhere to hide."
Bob Lauder, SOCA Regional Director for Scotland and Northern Ireland

Police officers enter a suspect's home as part of an organised crime unit raid. They hope to arrest key members of a drug gang.

A lot of organised crime involves criminals from different countries. To help police tackle this, there is a large international police organisation called Interpol. Interpol is based in Lyon, France, where officials from more than 80 different countries work together to combat international crime.

A police officer waits for the signal to arrest a drug dealer.

In Britain, organised crime is tackled by SOCA – the Serious Organised Crime Agency. Many of its officers have the combined powers of police, customs and immigration officers. Their main job is to gather intelligence (information) but they are also involved in making arrests.

AF FACTS

In the USA, organised crime is tackled by the FBI (Federal Bureau of Investigation). Its officers are called agents and they have authority above the police. They work across the USA gathering intelligence and making arrests. The FBI has around 33,652 employees.

Police detectives approach a suspect's car in New York.

Mission: Cocaine ring crushed

Cocaine is a highly addictive illegal drug. In April 2007, the Crown Prosecution Service convicted the head of an organised crime gang of bringing the drug into Britain.

A coca grower in Colombia checks his plants.

For years, a man called Karl Pettitt (opposite page) lived a life of luxury, paid for by the money he made smuggling cocaine into the UK. Pettitt lived in Spain, where he bought large quantities of cocaine from a Colombian gang. He then used his criminal contacts to smuggle it into the UK.

AF FACTS

Cocaine (below) is produced from the leaves of the coca plant, which grows in South America. Colombia produces 75% of the world's cocaine, and 90% of cocaine sold in the USA.

It took a lot of work by SOCA officers and the Spanish police to catch Pettitt, and to bring down his organised crime ring. By using recorded telephone conversations, they linked Pettitt to people who had already been arrested for selling large amounts of cocaine in the UK. Pettitt was sent to prison for 22 years.

"Karl Pettitt had been leading a lavish lifestyle off the back of his illegal profits. His sentencing ... marks the end of a serious organised criminal enterprise."
Ian Welch, CPS reviewing lawyer of the Organised

SWAT teams

SWAT stands for Special Weapons And Tactics. SWAT teams and other Special Operations units are trained to perform high-risk operations, such as hostage rescues.

Most SWAT teams are found in US police forces. SWAT officers are selected from volunteers already serving in the police. In order to qualify, they have to pass a number of mental and physical tests, and undergo special training. Among other things, they are taught marksmanship (shooting skill), first aid and **negotiation** tactics.

This German SWAT team is assault training using an armoured police vehicle.

POLIZEI

Helmet

Safety googles

Mask

Body armour

AR–15 assault rifle

POLICE

SWAT teams are very well armed and use submachine-guns such as the H & K MP5 and rifles including the Colt AR–15 and H & K G36. These compact weapons make them ideal for use inside buildings and in other confined spaces.

"I liked being part of the action. I have experienced what most officers will never in a lifetime – I would never change a day of it."

James Gnew, on his retirement from the Cleveland Police SWAT Unit

SWAT teams are transported in armoured vehicles.

DACORUM LRC

Mission: North Hollywood Shootout

On 28 February 1997, Los Angeles Police Department and LA County Sheriff's Department SWAT officers were involved in one of the most violent shootouts in US history.

Injured people hide behind a police car while officers open fire in the North Hollywood Shootout.

The North Hollywood Shootout began soon after 9 a.m. on what was a warm Friday morning. A passing police patrol car spotted two heavily armed men wearing body armour. The men entered the Bank of America branch on Laurel Canyon Boulevard. The police radioed for back up.

Police officers crouch down while the bank robbers fire back at them.

One of the masked bank robbers with a gun.

Inside the bank, shots were fired. As the men, Larry Phillips Jr and Emil Matasareanu, came out they found themselves surrounded by police. Phillips and Matasareanu began shooting at the officers as they tried to escape. When it became obvious that the police pistols and shotguns were not breaking through the bank robbers' armour, SWAT was called in. Eventually SWAT officers shot the gunmen, who both died at the scene.

"He never forgot where you were. If you shot at him, he'd just turn and spray fifty rounds at you." LAPD Sgt. Dean Haynes describes the encounter with Phillips before SWAT arrived

ACTION STATS

Phillips and Matasareanu were armed with five illegally modified fully automatic rifles, two Beretta 92F pistols, and a revolver. The rifles were loaded with armour-piercing bullets. During the shootout the two bank robbers fired about 1,300 rounds, injuring ten police officers and seven civilians.

Fast facts

There are just over 167,000 police officers in the the UK. Around 78% of those officers are men and 22% are women.

The Metropolitan Police in London is the largest police force in the UK, employing 20% of all the country's police officers.

The USA has around 883,600 police officers. The largest police force in the USA is the New York City Police Department, with around 37,800 officers – just over 4% of the total.

Australia's largest police force is the New South Wales Police Force, with around 15,500 officers. The state of New South Wales contains some of Australia's biggest cities, including Sydney and Melbourne.

The world's largest international police organisation is Interpol. It has 188 different member countries and exists to fight international crime, such as drug trafficking.

The world's largest police force is the Chinese People's Armed Police Force, with around 1.5 million officers. China is home to 1,325 million people, around a fifth of all the people on the planet.

Glossary

Abseil - to lower yourself down a rope on a harness, usually on a cliff face or steep slope.

Authority - the power to make decisions or to give orders.

Court - part of the legal system in which a suspect is put on trial in front of a judge and jury.

Demonstration - a crowd of people protesting at something they don't agree with.

DNA - deoxyribonucleic acid, found inside living cells of all living things.

Epicentre - the point where an earthquake first reaches the surface and where it is most violent and destructive.

Firearms - another word for guns.

Forensic - scientific tests used in the investigation of a crime.

Homicide - another word for murder, when one human is killed by another.

Negotiation - using communication to try to resolve a situation peacefully.

Rural - to do with the countryside; the opposite of urban (to do with towns and cities).

Scuba - equipment, including an air tank and face mask, which enables a person to breathe underwater.

Smuggling - to bring goods into a country illegally.

Surveillance - when people are closely watched and followed by the police. They record information by taking photographs and making notes.

Terrain - a type of ground and conditions, such as rocky hills.

Unique - individual; not like anything else.

Websites

www.policecouldyou.co.uk

This is the website to visit if you are thinking about joining the police in the UK. It also has information about becoming a police community support officer or a volunteer special constable.

www.police.uk/forces.htm

This page on the UK police website has links to the websites of all of Great Britain's territorial police forces.

www.met.police.uk

The home page of London's Metropolitan Police. Has links to all of the latest London police news stories.

www.police.govt.nz

The official website of the New Zealand Police.

www.police.nsw.gov.au

The website of the New South Wales Police Force, the largest police force in Australia.

www.gmp.police.uk

Website of the Greater Manchester Police, the second largest police force in the UK after the Metropolitan Police.

**www.nyc.gov/html/nypd/html/home/
home.shtml**

Official website of the New York City Police
Department, the biggest single police force in
the USA.

www.justice.gov/dea/index.htm

Internet home of the DEA, the United States'
Drug Enforcement Administration.

www.rcmp-grc.gc.ca

Website of the Royal Canadian Mounted Police.

www.interpol.int

The website of Interpol, the world's largest
international police organisation and a major
force in fighting drug trafficking and other forms
of organised crime.

www.soca.gov.uk

Home page of SOCA, Britain's Serious Organised
Crime Agency.

**Please note: every effort has been made by the Publishers to ensure that
these websites contain no inappropriate or offensive material. However,
because of the nature of the Internet, it is impossible to guarantee that
the contents of these sites will not be altered. We strongly advise that
Internet access is supervised by a responsible adult.**

Index